LET'S LOOK AT

EGYPT

BY MARY MEINKING

raintree
a Capstone company — publishers for children

Raintree is an imprint of Capstone Global Library Limited, a company incorporated in England and Wales having its registered office at 264 Banbury Road, Oxford, OX2 7DY – Registered company number: 6695582

www.raintree.co.uk
myorders@raintree.co.uk

Text © Capstone Global Library Limited 2020
The moral rights of the proprietor have been asserted.

All rights reserved. No part of this publication may be reproduced in any form or by any means (including photocopying or storing it in any medium by electronic means and whether or not transiently or incidentally to some other use of this publication) without the written permission of the copyright owner, except in accordance with the provisions of the Copyright, Designs and Patents Act 1988 or under the terms of a licence issued by the Copyright Licensing Agency, Barnard's Inn, 86 Fetter Lane, London, EC4A 1EN (www.cla.co.uk). Applications for the copyright owner's written permission should be addressed to the publisher.

Edited by Jessica Server
Designed by Juliette Peters
Picture research by Jo Miller
Production by Laura Manthe
Originated by Capstone Global Library Ltd
Printed and bound in India

ISBN 978 1 4747 8448 1 (hardback)
ISBN 978 1 4747 8465 8 (paperback)

British Library Cataloguing in Publication Data
A full catalogue record for this book is available from the British Library.

Photo Credits
Alamy: Jack Sullivan, 15; Newscom: Sipa USA/Xinhua, 18-19; Shutterstock: Adamsgraphy, 13, Amr mahmoud Soliman, 22-23, 24, Amy Nichole Harris, 11, Cat Downie, 8, eFesanko, Cover Top, 14, 17, Ewa Studio, Cover Middle, Cover Back, 6-7, Kanuman, Cover Bottom, Leonid Andronov, 1, nale, 4 (map), Orhan Cam, 20-21, paula french, 16, Photoonlife, 22 (Inset), Skreidzeleu, 4-5, Vladimir Wrangel, 9, WitR, 2-3

Every effort has been made to contact copyright holders of material reproduced in this book. Any omissions will be rectified in subsequent printings if notice is given to the publisher.

All the internet addresses (URLs) given in this book were valid at the time of going to press. However, due to the dynamic nature of the internet, some addresses may have changed, or sites may have changed or ceased to exist since publication. While the author and publisher regret any inconvenience this may cause readers, no responsibility for any such changes can be accepted by either the author or the publisher.

CONTENTS

Where is Egypt? 4
From deserts to rivers. 6
In the wild 8
People 10
At the table 12
At work 14
Transport 16
Festivals 18
Famous place 20

Quick Egypt facts 22
Glossary 22
Find out more 23
Comprehension questions 24
Index 24

Where is Egypt?

Egypt is in north-east Africa. It borders Asia. It is four times bigger than the United Kingdom. Egypt's capital city is Cairo.

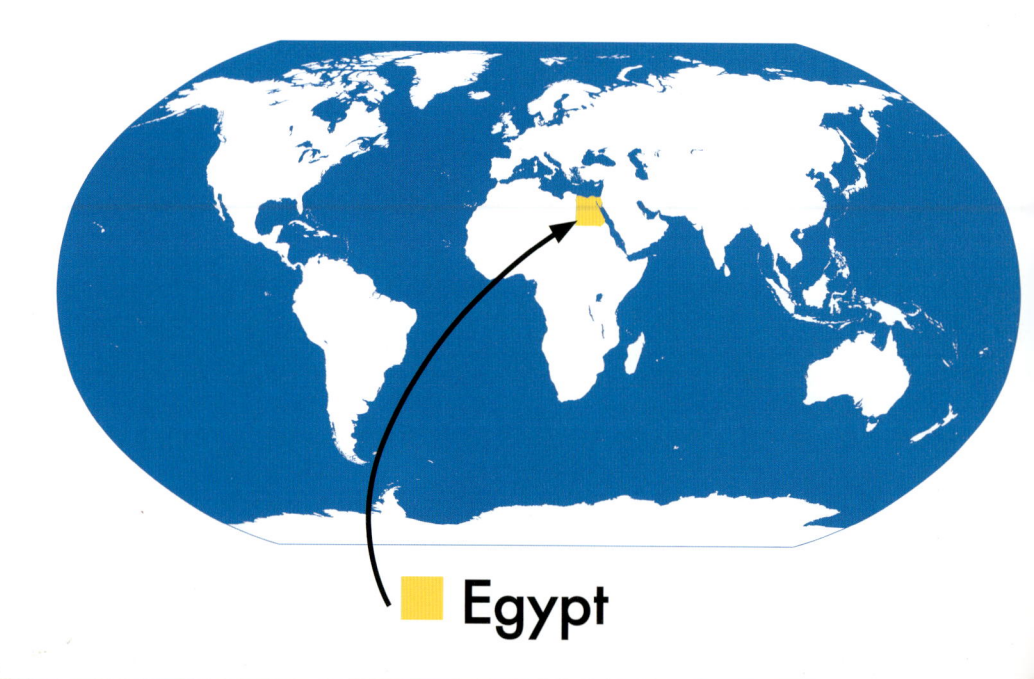

◼ Egypt

Cairo

From deserts to rivers

Most of Egypt is a desert. The air is hot and dry. The long River Nile cuts through the country. The Sinai Peninsula is an area in the east. It has high mountains.

River Nile

In the wild

Egypt's desert is home to gazelles, desert foxes and bearded sheep. Small foxes, rodents, lizards and snakes live there too.

desert fox

gazelle

People

Some Egyptian ancestors came from northern Africa. Others came from Asia, especially Arab lands. Today Egypt's official language is Arabic.

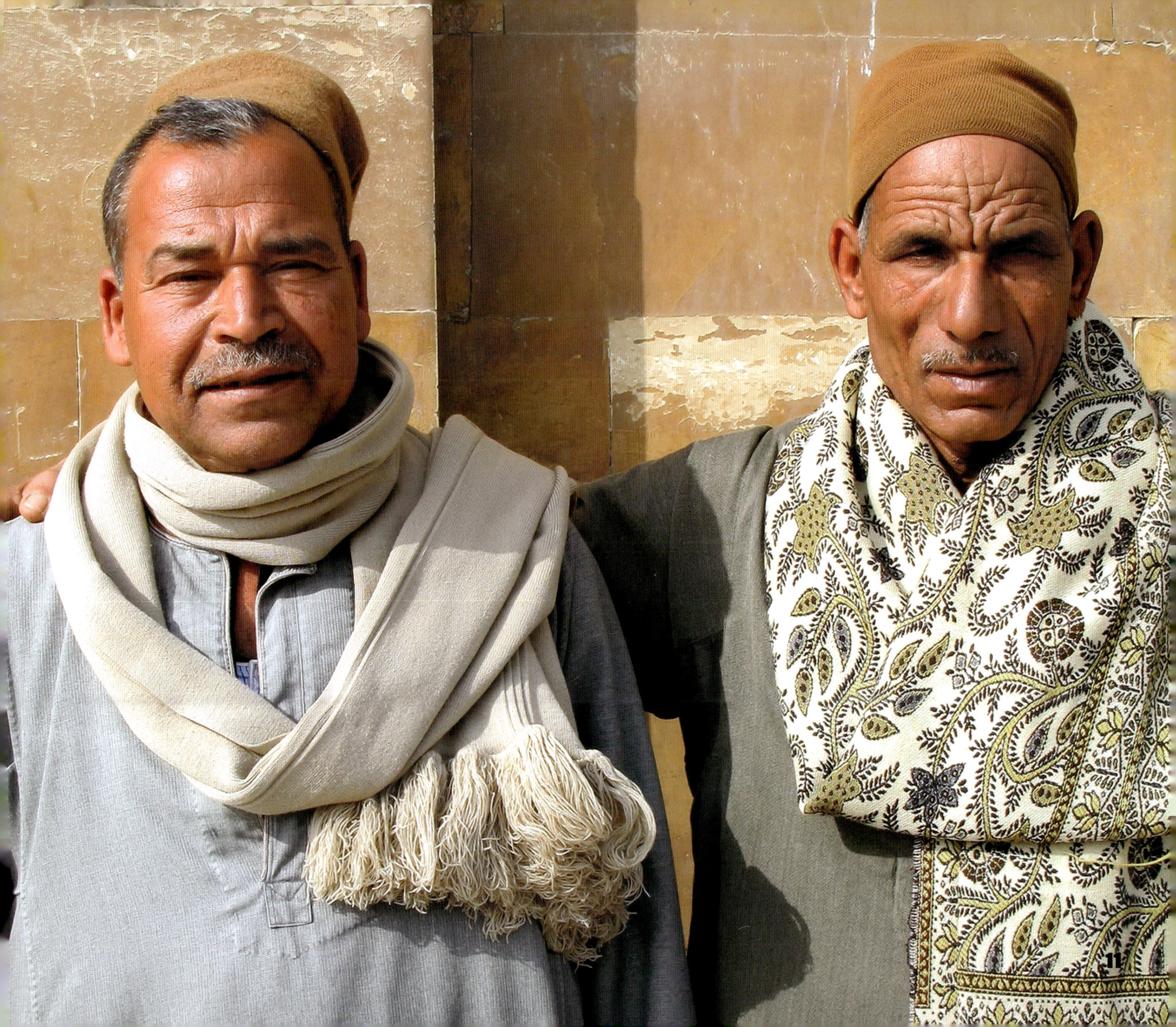

At the table

Vegetables, beans and fresh fruits are common foods in Egypt. People enjoy mashed beans called *ful*. They use flatbread to scoop up food. Egyptians drink sweet hot tea.

ful

At work

Many Egyptians are farmers. Others make crafts and fabrics. Some people help tourists as guides or drivers. Some work in museums and hotels.

rug weaving

Dan's nights at his small, quiet church have always been uneventful, filled with routine prayers and the occasional sinner seeking solace. But one evening, everything changes when a new visitor steps into the confessional—the Devil himself.

Claiming he wants to tell his side of the story, the Devil challenges everything Dan holds sacred. As the Prince of Darkness unravels the tales of his own fall and the true nature of sin, Dan finds himself questioning his faith, his beliefs, and the very fabric of good and evil as he listens to *the Morningstar CONFESSION*

Matthew Lutton crafts a dark and introspective narrative in The Morningstar Confession, blending theological musings with a haunting atmosphere that keeps readers questioning the boundaries between good, evil, and humanity's place in the universe.

— Steven Pajak, author of **THE DEVIL'S DOORWAY** and **THE HAUNTING OF ELENA VERA**

"Matt Lutton gives us a glimpse of humanity from an outsiders view, but what The Morningstar Confession really does is weaves a parable of loneliness, despair, and internalized suffering. This is a story about the beauty of being human, flaws and all. It's a psalm for our regrets. It's our confession. And it's a nod from the booth that we are forgiven."

— Gage Greenwood, author of **Bunker Dogs**

ISBN 9798991063333

15

Transport

People can travel by boat down the River Nile. Cairo has trams and an underground train system. In the countryside, people sometimes use donkeys to carry people or goods.

17

Festivals

One popular Egyptian festival is Sham el-Nessim. It is celebrated at the beginning of spring. Families go to parks or the countryside. They enjoy picnics and decorate colourful eggs.

19

Famous place

Egypt's most famous site is in Giza. There are three giant pyramids. They were built around 4,500 years ago. The Great Sphinx stone statue is nearby. It has the head of a person and the body of a lion.

21

QUICK EGYPT FACTS

Name: Arab Republic of Egypt
Capital: Cairo
Other major cities: Alexandria, Giza, and Shubra el-Kheima
Population: 99,413,317 (July 2018 estimate)
Size: 1,001,450 sq km (386,662 square miles)
Language: Arabic
Money: Egyptian pound

Egypt's flag

GLOSSARY

ancestor a family member who lived a long time ago

capital the city in a country where the government is based

metro a subway system in a city

peninsula a piece of land with water on three sides

pyramid a large, ancient Egyptian stone structure used as a tomb for a pharaoh

sphinx a creature with the body of a lion and a head of a person

FIND OUT MORE

Books

Egypt (Country Guides with Benjamin Blog), Anita Ganeri (Raintree, 2014)

Africa (Introducing Continents), Chris Oxlade and Anita Ganeri (Raintree, 2018)

See Inside Ancient Egypt (See Inside), Rob Lloyd Jones (Usborne, 2007)

Websites

Fun facts about the Pyramids at Giza
www.fun-facts.org.uk/wonders_of_world/pyramids_giza.htm

Search for "Egypt" at the National Geographic kids site to find out more
www.natgeokids.com/uk/

More information about Egypt
easyscienceforkids.com/all-about-egypt

COMPREHENSION QUESTIONS

1. Name some of Egypt's desert animals.

2. If you lived in Egypt, what type of job would you like? Why?

3. Most of the people in Egypt live along the River Nile. Why do you think that is?

INDEX

Africa 4, 10
animals 8
Asia 4, 10
capital 4
cities 4, 16, 20
deserts 6, 8
festivals 18

food 12
Great Sphinx 20
jobs 14
mountains 6
pyramids 20
rivers 6, 8, 16
transport 16